Readi- Set Go!

A Simple Guide to Establishing A Successful Small Business

STEPHANIE A.WYNN
AND JEFFREY WHITE

Published by Richter Publishing LLC
www.richterpublishing.com

Editors: Monica San Nicholas, Kati Scanlon, Katharina Jung

Book Cover Design: Jessie Alarcon

Library Control Numbers:

ISBN: 1945812052

ISBN-13: 9781945812057

DISCLAIMER

This book is designed to provide information on entrepreneurship only. This information is provided and sold with the knowledge that the publisher and author do not offer any legal or medical advice. In the case of a need for any such expertise, consult with the appropriate professional. This book does not contain all information available on the subject. This book has not been created to be specific to any individual people or organizations' situation or needs. Reasonable efforts have been made to make this book as accurate as possible. However, there may be typographical and or content errors. Therefore, this book should serve only as a general guide and not as the ultimate source of subject information. This book contains information that might be dated or erroneous and is intended only to educate and entertain. The author and publisher shall have no liability or responsibility to any person or entity regarding any loss or damage incurred, or alleged to have incurred, directly or indirectly, by the information contained in this book or as a result of anyone acting or failing to act upon the information in this book. You hereby agree never to sue and to hold the author and publisher harmless from any and all claims arising out of the information contained in this book. You hereby agree to be bound by this disclaimer, covenant not to sue and release. You may return this book within the guarantee time period for a full refund. In the interest of full disclosure, this book contains affiliate links that might pay the author or publisher a commission upon any purchase from the company. While the author and publisher take no responsibility for any virus or technical issues that could be caused by such links, the business practices of these companies and or the performance of any product or service, the author or publisher has used the product or service and makes a recommendation in good faith based on that experience.

All characters appearing in this work are fictitious. Any resemblance to real persons, living or dead, is purely coincidental.

DEDICATION

Stephanie A. Wynn

I would like to dedicate this book to my parents, Samuel Wynn and Diane M. Hines. Thank you for always encouraging me to be my very best. You were always there to straighten me out when I would get sidetracked. You corrected me even when I felt I was right. Your independence, resilience, work ethic, and sacrifices allowed me to be the person I am today. You have always been there for me no matter where I was in life. You always gave me advice on a spiritual and realistic level.

Life wasn't always perfect, but you made the very best of it. You always reminded me that there is always someone in line to take your place in every situation. You reminded me that no matter how negative people can be, that I should be better than that and make a difference. You encouraged me to help people without them even asking. If you see a need, fill the need. You instilled in me to never put money on anything I do, because if your heart is right, the money will come. You are the best parents that I could have ever asked for; your parenting made a difference in my life. You have supported every business venture, relocation, and supported the boys. You taught me to have a heart and keep God first. For that, I will be forever thankful and blessed. You are the epitome of what parents should be to their child. I love you, Mom and Dad.

ACKNOWLEDGMENTS

Stephanie A. Wynn

I would like to acknowledge God for placing the important people in my life at the designated time. Without God, nothing is possible. Jeremiah 29:11 says, *"For I know the plans I have for you."* You have always had a better plan and been faithful in my life. For that, I am forever blessed and thankful. For those who've had a hand in my success, I want to thank you for everything.

To my sons, Jamie and Brian: from the time you were born, I always wanted nothing but the very best for you. We have come far from where we were. You two have always been my motivation to keep pressing my way even when times were tough. I would think about you, and that was my spark to keep going and to make things happen. Always remember nothing is impossible and with God first, you cannot fail.

To my brothers Andre and Maurice: thank you for always listening when I needed to vent or just needed your opinion on situations. When times were difficult or seemed rough, you would tell me to *"Stay Gold, Pony Boy!"* when *"Staying Gold"* was all we had to hold on to.

To Jeffrey White, we have endured some trials and tribulations, and we maintained our friendship even if I was wrong. You always kept me focused on the straight and narrow. As you would say *"It's not if, it's when."* I have always kept that in my memory bank because that is a very true statement. We never took life for granted and we promised to remain focused on our dreams. We are living our dream.

To Shakira Webb and Rolanda King-Jones: we have been through what some will say is the impossible. We have stories and experiences that will last a lifetime. Through the trials and struggles we endured together as friends, we remained loyal and faithful no matter what the circumstances were. Our friendship has always been open and non-judgmental. We are so different yet so much alike.

To Antwan Jennings: who would have known that we would have come this far? We have fought, cried, laughed, and prayed for this very thing. You always told me to *"wake up every day and say 'good morning.'"* You always encouraged me never to give up on my goals and dreams. We fought through the dysfunction of life's challenges and always came out on top. I thank God for placing you in the right place at His designated time and for blessing our friendship.

ACKNOWLEDGEMENTS

Jeffrey White

I'd first like to thank God for His grace and mercy. With God, all things are possible! I'd also like to thank my son, Little Jeffrey, for keeping me focused and driven. I hope to inspire him to be the best he can be. I'd like to thank my wife Monica for supporting me as I took a leap of faith and quit my job to be my own boss. It hasn't been easy, but you stood by my side the entire time. Thank you, and I love you.

Lastly, I must thank Stephanie A. Wynn for giving me the opportunity to assist her with writing this wonderful book. I am honored to be chosen and happy to help you achieve your dreams. We have always supported each other since day one and will continue to as we climb the ladder of success. Together!

CONTENTS

Introduction: Getting Started 1

1: Why Do Businesses Fail? 3

2: Time Management 11

3: What Type of Business Are You? 21

4: Creating Your Brand 27

5: Building Your Team.. 37

6: Getting the Support You Need 50

7: Social Media and Your Business 53

8: The Art of Professionalism.. 62

9: No Discounts: Perception is Everything.................... 67

10: Logic vs. Emotion 74

11: Tax Write-Offs.. 78

12: Saving For Retirement 82

13: Investment Options 87

14: Closing Remarks.. 90

ABOUT THE AUTHORS 96

INDEX 99

INTRODUCTION:
GETTING STARTED

Congratulations! If you're reading this, it means you're either interested in starting a business or have recently started one. My name is Stephanie A. Wynn, and along with Jeffrey White, we are going to provide you with some great tips on how to create a successful small business with simple, easy-to-use methods that have withstood the test of time. Starting a business can be overwhelming and a little discouraging at times, but with careful planning, preparation, and hard work, your business venture can be a successful one too.

I have had two successful businesses ventures in my life thus far: an ice cream shop and a cleaning business. Even though these are two vastly different endeavors, I discovered that they both followed a similar business plan. Instead of reinventing the wheel and doing things I wasn't sure would work, I applied tried and true concepts and business practices that have worked for countless others.

Before embarking on your business journey, it's important to be mentally prepared for the challenges that lie ahead. You must go in with the clear understanding that running a successful business takes a lot of work and mental toughness. Things can be going great one day and then be falling apart the next. Keeping your emotions in check is critical.

In this book, we will provide the blueprint for business success and discuss why it's important to understand *why* businesses fail. Avoiding pitfalls is critical to success.

1

WHY DO BUSINESSES FAIL?

It is estimated that nine out of ten business start-ups fail within the first five years. Our goal is to ensure that you're one of the successful 10%.

There are many reasons why businesses fail. Here are the top reasons why and the ways to overcome them:

1. **Letting your emotions take control.** There are many factors in running a successful business, and being mentally strong is at the top of the list. Two things that helped me tremendously (and still do to this day) are prayer and meditation. Meditation helped me stay calm during times of crisis. It also helped me clear my mind and gave me clarity on issues and challenges I was unsure of. The ability to block out the negativity and stay focused is essential if we want to succeed in anything.

Prayer helped me to stay grounded and have faith in myself and my abilities even when no one else would. When times were tough, I would refer to my favorite scripture: *"I can do all things through Christ who strengthens me"* (Philippians 4:13). When things aren't going your way, and you don't know what to do, just start praying.

2.   Lack of support. A strong support system is key for successful start-ups. You need a support system that will keep you motivated and focused on the task at hand. You're going to need all the positive energy and encouragement you can muster to withstand the challenging times that most business owners face.

Running a business means living with uncertainty on a daily basis and not having a steady paycheck. If most of your friends work a typical nine-to-five job, they may be uncomfortable with the lack of structure and long hours with little reward that you as a small business owner will deal with when starting out. (They may not tell you this, but it's an important point to remember when seeking advice from them).

As a small business owner, it's important to understand that not everyone will agree with your vision. They may not understand why you're working so hard with little to show for it. It's important to surround yourself with people who will support you, even if they don't understand you.

People will often tell you to *follow your dreams*, but they want those dreams to be well-paying and stable. Unfortunately, the dreams with the biggest rewards often don't fit into this category. Don't let their lack of support or understanding discourage you from your dreams.

3. **Not listening to the customer.** I recently met with a gentleman to discuss some services he offered. Even though I asked him very specific questions about what I was looking for, he instead proceeded to tell me about services I was not interested in. I felt as though he didn't listen to what I wanted, but wanted to tell me what he thought I needed. I didn't need those items, nor did he give me a chance to tell him so. Needless to say, he lost a potentlal customer because he was so focused on the wrong things.

It's imperative that you listen to your customer. Too many entrepreneurs have an idea, but fail to determine whether there's demand for that idea or product. Give them what *they* want, not what you want to sell them or *think* they want.

4. **Too much like everyone else.** The key to being successful is to be unique and stand out from the competition. What makes you or your product different? Why should they spend money with you instead of choosing other similar products out there? If you want to be successful, you must stand out from the crowd.

5. **No business plan.** The old adage *"Failing to plan is planning to fail"* is true. To have a successful business, you must have a plan. If a person is driving to a place they've never been, they will get directions. Pilots have a flight plan. Seamen have navigation systems. Without a course of direction, they are sure to get lost. The same rationale applies to running a business: to reach your destination, you must have a plan to get there.

Other reasons to create a business plan include the following:

- Having a clear statement of your vision and mission

- Clearly identify your customers and their buying habits

- Details of your market strategies

- Contingency plans for "what if" scenarios

- Analysis of your industry, your competition, and ways to compete

These are just a few reasons to have a business plan. We will discuss business plans in more detail in an upcoming chapter.

6.   Failure to delegate. It can be difficult for business owners to delegate duties to others, but it is something they must learn to do. One person cannot do everything, even though they will try. Spreading yourself too thin can compromise productivity, which can affect the bottom line (aka profits).

7.   Fear of success. Yes, this is real. The fear of success was first diagnosed in the 1970's by psychologist Matina Horner. Her findings were questioned at the time, but today they are widely accepted.

Classic symptoms of fearing success include the following:

- You feel guilty about success because those close to you aren't doing as well as you

- You self-sabotage your work

- You believe if you achieve success you won't be able to maintain it

- Deep down, you believe you don't deserve it

- You avoid telling those close to you about your business to avoid conflict or feelings of animosity toward you

Do you experience any of these symptoms? If so, you may have a fear of success.

9. **An unconscious incompetent.** This is a person who thinks they know everything. As a result, they don't make an effort to learn anything new or listen to feedback that may be beneficial to the growth of their business. In other words, this person is not aware that they lack the necessary knowledge.

No one knows everything. There is a lot you don't know about your industry. Would you feel comfortable going to a lawyer, doctor, or dentist who'd stopped reading trade journals because they graduated from their respective institutions ten years ago? How effective would a computer programmer be if he/she did not study the new technological advances?

It's the same philosophy with you and your business.

No matter how much you think you know, you should study and monitor the trends of your industry. Take small business classes or entrepreneurial courses at your local city chamber of commerce. Attend small business networking seminars and mixers. This will give you an opportunity to interact with other business owners and learn things that can benefit you.

These sessions are very informative and can give you the motivation to press forward with your business venture. I am a true believer that if you surround yourself with successful business minded people, you will eventually become successful as well. The more you know about your industry, the greater your probability of success is.

10. **Lack of advertising.** To cut costs or keep expenses low, many business owners will spend less on advertising. This may save money, but how will people know who you are if you don't advertise? Advertising can range from the very expensive (30-second Super Bowl ads) to free (talking about your business on Facebook or Twitter). When it comes to business, the old adage *"If you build it, they will come"* does not apply anymore. Instead, live by the motto *"If the baby don't cry, the baby don't eat."*

11. **Starting for the wrong reason.** Many people get tired of working for someone else and decide to quit their job and strike out on their own. In the beginning a person may be full of enthusiasm and excitement about running a business, but it's hard work. A great example is exercise: in January, a person may commit to working out daily to lose weight, but by February, they give up.

They soon realize it requires much more work than they anticipated and they don't see any results. Running a business is the same way. Excitement soon wears off, and people quickly realize it will take much more effort than anticipated. It takes more than excitement and emotions to make a successful business.

Knowing why businesses fail is key to avoiding these pitfalls and not becoming a statistic. In which of these areas do you feel the weakest? Identify your problem areas and strengthen them accordingly.

In the next section, we'll discuss another important subject for small business owners, which is time management.

2

TIME MANAGEMENT

As a small business owner, you will be pulled in many different directions. It may be a challenge, but being able to manage your time is a must.

I cannot express this enough: time management skills are the key to being successful in any endeavor. This isn't just a business philosophy, it applies to life as well. No matter what type of business you're starting, you must learn to prioritize your time. That old saying *"time is money"* is true. You will miss out on many opportunities if you do not have time management skills.

Each and every minute of the day must count. Here are a few things that can help you maximize your time:

Create a Vision Board

The vision board is just that: your vision of what you can see happening for yourself. I often say that God gives you a vision and the provisions to make them come true. A trifold board allows you to create an easily accessible vision board that you can put anywhere:

By writing down your vision and goals and reading them daily, your subconscious mind will begin to find ways to make them come true. Even if the path isn't obvious right now, events and circumstances will begin to happen to make them a reality. This will give you a clear picture of your vision as a business owner and can help you to stay focused on your goals.

How to create a vision board:

My vision board is composed of a tri-fold board with three columns and three topics:

1st Column

- **Short-term goals:** These tasks are accomplished in the near term (usually a couple of weeks or months).

2nd (Middle) Column

- **Accomplishments:** These are the projects, tasks or milestones that have been completed successfully.

3rd column

- **Long-term goals:** These are the long-range plans that are made up of short-term goals. Long-term goals are usually several months to several years down the road. For example, a start-up wanting to be a Fortune 500 company in 5-10 years is a long-term goal.

Each morning, you should review your board and make any necessary adjustments.

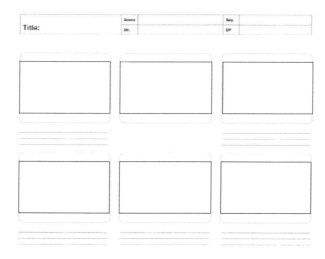

- **Post-it notes:** Write your thoughts on a post-it note and add it to your vision board. To reinforce these thoughts, I place them on my vision board and bedroom mirror as well. Everywhere I turn, I see my goals and visions. This helps me to stay focused and decrease negative thoughts that may creep into my mind.

Here are a few vision board success stories:

- After getting booed offstage at an LA comedy club, a dejected young Jim Carey went home and wrote himself a check for $10 million. In the memo section, he wrote: *"For acting services rendered."* The rest is history.

- Ellen DeGeneres used a vision board to realize

her dream of appearing on the cover of *"O"* Magazine.

- Katy Perry made a vision board as a fourth grader, using a photo of Selena accepting a Grammy award. While Katy hasn't won a Grammy yet, she has won many other awards and has been nominated 15 times.

- On the morning of the presidential election, November 4, 2008, Oprah called New York City radio station Power 105.1 and shared the following story:

I was speaking with Michelle [Obama] and Caroline Kennedy and Maria Shriver – we were all doing a big rally out in California. At the end of the rally Michelle Obama said something powerful: '...I want you to leave here and envision Barack Obama taking the oath of office'. I created a vision board. I had never had a vision board before. I came home, I got me a board and put Barack Obama's picture on it, and I put a picture of my dress I want to wear to the inauguration."

In each of these instances, they just had a vision and nothing else. They weren't close to achieving these lofty goals, but with hard work and patience, their subconscious mind eventually got them there.

When traveling to a place you've never been, it's a good idea to have a set of directions handy in case you get lost or turned around. A vision board works the same way. Starting a business often means going someplace you've never been before. The vision board can keep you on track and on a set course to your final destination.

This is the power of visualization. Most people are visual and tend to believe what they see. The key is to create visions with as much detail as possible: Imagine you're actually in the moment. What are you wearing? What time of day is it? Who is around as it is occurring? Are you wearing cologne? What does it smell like?

The more realistic the vision, the greater the probability of it coming true.

The Mission Statement: What will be Your Mission?

The mission statement is an excellent resource to help business owners stay focused on the goals and objectives of the company. Here are the top reasons to have a mission statement:

- **It helps with decision making.** It's easy to make decisions if a mission statement has been drafted. If a business opportunity does not assist with the goals of the company, it can be quickly rejected.

- **It focuses on the company's future.** Mission statements can prevent a company from getting sidetracked by things that won't help the company long term.

- **It determines the company's direction.** Mission statements are the road map that all businesses must follow.

Mission statements are usually one page or less in length. There are no set guidelines, but there are a few key questions most mission statements will answer:

- What is the business of the organization?
- What type or level of service is provided?
- What are the core beliefs and values?
- What are the needs of its customers, and how will the company satisfy them?

By answering these questions, a person will have a clear and concise mission statement to refer to time and time again.

The Business Plan

A business plan should be the summary of the future plans you have for your business. Most business plans are used when attempting to obtain loans or financing from banks. It's always a good idea to have your business plan updated and readily available when attempting to get funding for your business. Your business plan should include the following:

- **Cover page:** This page will include the company name and business logo.

- **Executive summary:** This is a well-written summary to grab the attention of your audience (i.e., bank/loan officer, investor's, etc.).

- **Company overview:** The company overview is a summary that reports the most important information about the company.

- **Industry analysis:** This gives a brief overview of the industry that your business is in.

- **Customer analysis:** In this section of the business plan, customers are analyzed along with their needs, wants, and whether or not your business is equipped to meet those demands.

- **Operation plan:** The operation plan is used to justify the operating budget. It details what it will take to support the strategic objectives of the company.

- **Management team:** The management team includes a list of senior management and their roles in the organization.

- **Financial plan:** The financial plan is a detailed evaluation of a company's current and future financial standings. This is used to predict future income assets and withdrawal plans.

- **Advertising, marketing plan, and budget:** The company advertising plans are detailed here, along with the budgets for these endeavors.

- **Expenses:** All known expenses of the business are listed here.

- **Grand opening expenses:** Any expenses related to the opening of the business are reported here.

- **Short-term goals:** Short-term goals are usually within 3-6 months and can include advertising, revenue, customer service, website traffic, etc. Short-term goals are designed to help the business reach long- term goals.

- **Long-term goals:** Long-term goals are usually six months to over a year away. Examples of long-term goals are doubling sales revenue next year, increasing customer satisfaction by 50% in twelve months, or increasing website traffic by 30% in one year.

Creating a business plan can be time-consuming and intimidating. As a result, some business owners opt to skip creating a plan, but this could be a mistake. Palo Alto Software conducted a study that asked thousands of small business owners about their businesses, goals and business planning. The responses showed that those who completed business plans were almost twice as likely to successfully grow their business or obtain capital compared to those who didn't write a plan.

The researchers concluded:

"Except in a small number of cases, business planning appeared to be positively correlated with business success as measured by our variables. While our analysis cannot say that completing a business plan will lead to success, it does indicate that the type of entrepreneur who completes a business plan is also more likely to run a successful business."[1]

Creating a business plan should be a top priority. It will provide the blueprint to creating a successful business. Remember: *Failing to plan means planning to fail.*

3

WHAT TYPE OF BUSINESS ARE YOU?

There are several types of business entities to choose from. Here are the most common types and the advantages and disadvantages of each.

- A sole proprietor may be ideal for those who are starting a small home business where expansion or large cash flows are expected for the foreseeable future.

- A partnership might be an option for two or more individuals who are forming a small business similar to the one described for a sole proprietorship.

- Individuals who are concerned about lawsuits or debt accrued under the business should consider opening an LLC.

- Corporations are an option for those who wish to issue stock in their company. Another reason is that the company is extremely profitable and you want to take advantage of lower tax rates. Having a corporation also gives family business owners the ability to gift ownership of the company as part of an estate, or to the next generation of owners without giving up control.

Business Types	Characteristics	Advantages	Disadvantages
Sole Proprietorship	One individual or a married couple in business	Complete control and decision making Few business requirements	Personally liable for all debts and obligations Limited ability to raise capital
General Partnership	Two or more individuals who contribute to the success of a business	Easy to establish Owners receive all profits, personal income taxes paid on profits	Each partner is liable for business debts and obligations One partner can't transfer their interests without consent of the other partners
Limited Liability Company (LLC)	One or more individuals formed by written agreement	Profits pass through the LLC and taxes are paid by owners Corporations and partnerships can be members	May be difficult to form
Corporation	A company or group authorized to act as a single entity legally	Shareholders not liable for debts or judgements	Must file Articles of Incorporation Shareholders can have a dominant voice over direction of business

Once you decide on the type of business you want, the following steps must be completed:

1. **Register your business and business name.** This enables you to open bank accounts, apply for loans and perform other duties under the business name.

2. **Apply for a federal employer identification number (EIN.)** Many sole proprietors opt to use their social security number while other business entities have an EIN.

3. **State and local business licenses.** Most businesses will need a city, county, or state license to operate within those jurisdictions.

4. **Organizational paperwork.** LLC's, partnerships and corporations all have paperwork that must be completed.

5. **Sales Tax license.** This applies to retail establishments.

6. **Business permits.** Certain businesses will require permits:

    o Sellers

    o Building

    o Health

    o Zoning

    o Home occupation

The type of permit needed will be dictated by the type of business being established.

7.   **Tax Forms.** All businesses (except partnerships) must file an annual income tax return. The form used will depend on how the company is organized. The following are common federal business and tax forms:

  o I-9: Employment Eligibility and Verification Form

  o SS-4: Employer ID Number (EIN) Application Form

  o W-2: Wage and Tax Statement Form

  o W-4: Employee's Withholding Allowance Certification Form

  o W-9: Taxpayer Identification Number and Certification Form

  o 1040 Schedule C (C-EZ): Profit or Loss from Business (Sole Proprietorship) Form

  o 1099 MISC: Miscellaneous Income Form

Many of these forms can be found online and completed there as well.

This is just a brief overview of what a person may or may not need depending on their type of business. Consulting a business or tax advisor is advised if a person is unsure of which form to use and when. It is important to know what is needed because the IRS will require these forms whether a person is aware of them or not.

Having your paperwork in order and up-to-date is critical to the success of your business.

4

CREATING YOUR BRAND

For your business to be a success, it must be unique and stand out from the rest of your competition. The goal is to create a distinctive style that will define the services that your small business will provide. One way to do this is by establishing your brand.

The Logo. A business logo is a must-have. Here are a few tips to consider when creating your business logo:

- **Make it difficult to forget.** Your logo is the first thing a client or consumer sees when it comes to your business. Your logo is what makes you memorable, and can either make you or break you. For example, children all over the world recognize McDonald's golden arches. Coca-Cola,

Walmart, Nike and Mercedes-Benz have famous logos that are easily recognizable. The goal is to create a logo that people won't forget.

- **Create a professional image.** Having an unprofessional looking logo gives the impression that your company is not to be taken seriously. In other words, a cheap logo can signify shoddy business practices and a business to be avoided at all costs. This can cause you to lose business before you've uttered a single word.

- **Keep the colors modest.** Keeping the colors simple and the detail not too intricate will help your logo appear the same everywhere it is used. Your logo may appear on a variety of platforms (television, billboards, print media, clothing, pens, etc.). Too much color or too many features may appear distorted or look differently from one type of media to the next. Keeping it simple is key.

- **Use it everywhere.** Make sure to put your logo on everything related to your business. It will take time for people to remember you or take notice. Brand recognition is key.

- **Business cards.** Once you have a logo, it's time to create a business card. Keep it simple. Business cards should be able to be read quickly. A person should not have to squint because

there's too much information on the card or the
font is too small. The front of your card should
have basic information in a quick, easy to read
format:

- o   Logo
- o   Your name
- o   What you do (job title)
- o   Contact info (address, phone number,
      email address)
- o   Website
- o   QR code

Note: the back of business cards is usually left blank,
but if you choose to add something to the back, make
sure the info is non-essential: mission statement,
tagline, etc.

The Final Checklist

Here is a handy final checklist reference chart. This is
a great way to gauge where you are with your business
and what needs to be completed next:

Business Cards	Easy-to-read cards with a brief summary of your business name and contact information.
Business Checking Account	Account where all of your small business financial transactions take place (deposits, withdrawals, etc.).
Business Website	Your website will display the products and services you provide.

Business Logo	Your logo is your brand and introduction to the world. Make it unforgettable.
Business Domain Name	This is www.Nameofyourbusiness.com. Purchasing your domain name is a wise business decision. This way, you will prevent someone from taking your business name and profiting at your expense.
The Entity	Are you a sole proprietor, limited liability company (LLC), s-corporation, c-corporation, or partnership? Choose the entity that best suits your business needs and goals. Selecting an entity will protect your personal assets/liabilities from your business assets/liabilities.
Marketing and Advertising	Effective marketing and advertising are critical to the success of your business. Popular marketing and advertising outlets include radio, social media outlets, local newspapers, local schools, television ads, and billboards.
Business Physical Location	Where will your business be located? Will you have a virtual office or physical address? **Note:** If you are homebased business owner, please make sure you have all of the required licensure to run a business from home.
Tax Advisor	Hiring a competent and reputable tax accountant is a wise investment decision. Many businesses run into

	problems with the IRS due to inefficient bookkeeping.
Business Email	Having a business email that ends with your **business name** as opposed to a personal email (Gmail, Yahoo, Hotmail, etc.) gives your business a more professional appearance.
Post-it Notes	Keep post-it notes handy to write down your thoughts and post them on your mirror or vision board.
411 Lookup	Having your business available on major search engines (i.e., Google, Bing, Yahoo, etc.) is key to attracting new business.
Business Telephone & Fax Number	Establishing a business telephone and fax number will help keep your personal information separate from your business.

The final checklist may seem like a lot, but many of these tasks can be completed within a short period of time. As a business owner, one of the most important phrases to remember is *"time is money."* The longer it takes to get these essentials taken care of, the less time you can spend servicing your clients and making money.

Key Questions

There are questions every business should periodically ask themselves to ensure that they are moving in the right direction:

1. What will set my business apart from other businesses?

    _____

    _____

    _____

2. What are my short-term goals for my business?

    _____

    _____

    _____

3. What are my long-term goals for my business?

    _____

    _____

    _____

4. Are we relevant? Will we be relevant five years from now? Ten years from now?

    _____

    _____

    _____

5. Will people want to work with me? Why or why not?

    _____

    _____

    _____

    _____

6. Am I paying enough attention to detail? What can be improved?

_____

_____

_____

7. What is stopping me from being a better boss?

_____

_____

_____

8. What program should I discontinue? What can be expanded?

_____

_____

_____

9. What are my educational and experience weaknesses? What can I do to improve them?

_____

_____

_____

10. Am I doing anything that goes against my personal beliefs for the sake of the business?

_____

_____

_____

11. Do I have the best people working with me? Who are they and why?

_____

_____

_____

12. How can I get more clients to like and trust me?

_____

_____

_____

13. Am I using technology up to its full potential to benefit my business?

_____

_____

_____

14. Is there any business I will turn down? If so, what type?

_____

_____

_____

15. What is the demographic of my clients? Has it changed over time or remained the same?

_____

_____

_____

16. Who are the three people I can turn to for advice and guidance?

_____

_____

_____

17. What keeps me inspired to keep going?

_____

_____

_____

18. Have I reached capacity, or is there room for additional growth?

_____

_____

_____

19. Is my website easy to navigate?

_____

_____

_____

20. What keeps me up at night worrying? How can I resolve the issue?

_____

_____

_____

These questions are designed to keep you focused on what's important.

By being frank and honest with yourself, you are one step closer to ensuring success.

5

BUILDING YOUR TEAM

In this chapter, we will discuss two important aspects of your business: your business team and your support team. Each will play a vital role in your business and can determine if your business will be a success or a failure.

As entrepreneurs, we are mentally prepared to do EVERYTHING. This is our company, and if we want something done, we must do it ourselves. While few people can argue with this notion, the fact of the matter is this: everyone needs help, and this is especially true of entrepreneurs. There are only so many hours in the day and entrepreneurs can't do it all, even if they believe they can. There are two primary ways that entrepreneurs get the help they need. One way is by outsourcing.

Outsourcing 101

There are two things all entrepreneurs and business owners must accept:

1. They don't *know* everything.
2. They can't *do* everything.

Once they can accept these facts of life, they may be more receptive to seeking help. One of the easiest ways to obtain much-needed help is by outsourcing.

In its simplest terms, outsourcing is paying someone not affiliated with your company to perform functions for the company. There are many ways to outsource. Some of the most popular options include the following:

Legal services:
Many start-up companies can't afford to hire an attorney or legal staff to handle their affairs (they may not need one, either). However, an expert may be needed to review the occasional legal documentation, contracts or litigation support.

Accounting and tax preparation:
Many entrepreneurs can save valuable time by

having their financial matters taken care of by experts in the field. Another perk is that these financial experts can help them save money by finding tax deductions and tax breaks.

Creative services:
Ghostwriters, graphic designers and marketing experts can be used on an as-needed basis.

Web design:
Having a well-designed, professional-looking website is mandatory in today's society. It must be easy-to-navigate and load quickly as well. A 2015 Radware Report found that 57% of site visitors will abandon a web page if it takes three seconds or longer to interact with key content.

Data entry:
Many entrepreneurs would rather pay someone than to perform mundane tasks such as scanning documents, processing orders or updating spreadsheets.

Phone support:
Phone support is a great option for businesses owners who don't have the manpower (or time) to receive a large volume of phone calls.

Manufacturing:
T-shirts, coffee mugs and other products with the

company logo are commonly outsourced. Larger, more established companies also outsource the building of many of their products as well.

For the busy entrepreneur, there are several reasons to consider outsourcing some of your business needs:

Benefits of Outsourcing

Time:
By outsourcing a few tasks, time can be spent doing other things that need time or special attention.

Reduced operating costs:
By hiring someone on an as-needed basis, operating expenses are drastically reduced.

Improved goods and services:
Outsourcing gives small businesses access to professional experts that help their business remain competitive with larger more established companies.

Decreased red tape:
Intricate details of complicated jobs can be avoided by outsourcing to qualified and licensed individuals.

Attempting to do everything can be counterproductive and detrimental to the success of your business. Working hard is important, but working smart is better.

Personally, I have outsourced projects and tasks to the following professions and professionals over the years:

- Publisher
- Journalist/Writer/Author
- Personal Trainer
- Barber
- Photographer
- Web-designer
- Property Manager
- Tax Advisor
- Advertising (logo and flyers)

Doing this saved me a lot of time, energy and stress. I knew these tasks were in capable hands and I was free to focus on other tasks.

By outsourcing tasks when needed, the busy entrepreneur can ensure their business has the look and feel of quality they desire. Outsourcing is one way to build your business team, and another is to hire quality people to complement your skills.

Business Partners: Can Friends Be Good Business Partners?

Many times, we will start businesses with people we know. This can be both a blessing and a curse. We usually have a comfort level with our friends where we trust them with things we hold dear to us. On the flipside, that friendship can cause tension when things aren't going well in the business.

The key with working with friends is to create a team of like-minded individuals who share your vision, work ethic and goals. This will help make your journey a lot less stressful.

Whether you opt for a friend or someone new, here are the top things to look for in a business partner:

1.   Discover your strengths and weaknesses.

What are you good at?

Where will you need the most assistance?

What aspects will you want to have more control over?

It's important you know this about yourself and to ensure your potential business partner knows this too.

2.   Get to know them personally. Spend some time away from work with your potential business partner and get to know them.

Do they have any habits you don't like that could impact the business?

Do they drink too much? Associate with unscrupulous people?

---

3. **Create an opt-out clause.** Consider creating a contract that dissolves after a certain time if things aren't working out. If the business relationship is working, great. If not, it dissolves cleanly and quickly.

4. **Get on the same page.** Make sure all business partners understand what the short and long-term goals of the business are, and everyone is in basic agreement on how to make them happen. Disagreements now could be a sign of more disagreements and heated arguments later.

5. **Get references:** Past employers, business partners, clients and friends can give a great assessment of your future business partner. Trust your gut and don't ignore any red flags that may appear.

I have learned over the years that you need a

business partner who will handle your business when you are not able to do so. No matter what industry your business is in, you need a reliable partner that you can trust. They have to be reliable and able to get work done at all times.

Always remember one important tidbit of info: everyone you started your business journey with may not complete the ride with you. Many friendships have ended because they started working together and things fell apart. Some may even stop communicating with you all together.

This is why it's important to choose your business partners wisely. In many instances, you will need their expertise to get jobs done. In other cases, outsourcing assignments may be the best option. When starting out you may think you can do it on your own, but you quickly realize that help is needed to make your dreams come true.

The Social Support Team

In addition to the business support system, the social support system is extremely important. Business partners and outsourcing can help keep the business running, but friends and family help with the intangibles.

Running a business takes a tremendous amount of

time, energy, effort and money. This is where the social support system comes in.

As a business owner, it's important to have a support system that understands this. Not everyone has the entrepreneurial spirit or understands the sacrifice it takes to run a business.

Social support tends to follow a pattern:

- **Inception.** people are generally supportive. They encourage you to pursue your dreams and tell you that you can do it.

- **Six months later.** the excitement and enthusiasm start to wane if business hasn't picked up.

- **One year later.** If business still hasn't picked up, some will suggest giving up or quitting.

- **Eighteen months or more.** At this point, many will question your sanity. They can't understand WHY you're working so hard with little result.

Listening to this type of dialogue is very dangerous for the entrepreneur and should be avoided for several reasons:

1. In many instances, it will take much more

effort than was originally projected to establish a successful business. Some estimate it can take up to five years or more for a business to become successful.

2. The average person does not want to own their own business. They prefer a guaranteed paycheck for a sense of security. There is absolutely nothing wrong with this, but this thought process can prevent them from seeing things from your perspective as an entrepreneur and business owner.

3. We live in a society where if things aren't completed within a specified time frame, it wasn't meant to be. Too often people will give up too soon and move on to a new project. The average person will believe if you aren't successful after a certain amount of time has passed, then it's time to give up.

Entrepreneurs and many in their social support system will have a different mindset when it comes to business. You must keep this in mind when seeking advice or encouragement from those who are not inclined to run their own business. Advice might be given from their personal perspective, which is much different from yours.

This can cause you to question your efforts and

second guess yourself if you are told something that goes against what you believe in your heart:

"It wasn't meant to be."
"At least you tried."
"Maybe it's time to get a 'real' job."

Many people are encouraged to follow their dreams, provided those dreams pay a nice salary on day one. There's one small problem: it could be *years* before those dreams become profitable. In other words, those dreams could take longer than your social support system are willing to wait. Many famous companies took years to make a profit: Federal Express, Apple Computers, and ESPN all took over five years to become successful.

There are two points that must be made here: not only does your social support team have to understand this, but you must accept this as well. It is a good idea to have a talk with your support team to let them know what expect from your business venture. Here are a few tips:

1.   **Focus on the long-term.** Tell them it may take longer than anticipated to make the business a success. You will need them to stay focused on the long-term and not get caught up in the day-to-day activities.

2.   **Be prepared for highs and lows.** Running a

business can be an emotional rollercoaster. There will be times of great joy and tremendous frustration or disappointment. It's par for the course.

3.   **Moral support.** During times of duress, the social support team will be needed to provide words of encouragement and uplift.

Having a strong social support system is essential to your business success. By simply offering moral support they can give you the push you need to keep going.

Beware of Fake Support

There's one aspect of the social support system that must be recognized, and that's the person who secretly *wants* you to fail. These are the people who will tell you it won't work and suggest that you should give up every time they are given the opportunity.

There are many reasons why they don't want you to succeed, but they may not involve you:

- They are jealous of your success.
- They take joy in seeing other people unhappy.
- They do not believe you deserve success.
- They do not think what you're trying to accomplish is worth it.

This can be the person you least expect: your best friend, sibling, spouse, or even your parents. It's important to remember that their limitations are not your limitations. Don't internalize their negative feelings toward you or let them deter you from accomplishing your goals. As we discussed in the previous section, they may not have an entrepreneurial spirit and understand what you're trying to do.

Remember: *this is YOUR life, and only you can live it.* Keep these negative people at arm's length because they can prevent you from being successful. Stay focused on your goals and don't let anyone stop you from making your business a successful one.

6

GETTING THE SUPPORT YOU NEED

Starting a business is not an easy task and can be made that much harder if the entrepreneur feels alone or has no support system. It's very important to avoid those who will discourage you as described in the previous chapter and associate with those who will motivate and encourage you instead.

The following groups and organizations are excellent options for those seeking mentors, guidance and encouragement:

Chambers of Commerce. Most cities have several chambers of commerce. These are organizations that allow business owners in the community to meet, share ideas and gain business contacts. Many chambers have programs and workshops for new business owners as well. www.chamberofcommerce.com.

Service Corps of Retired Executives. SCORE is a group of retired businessmen and executives who give free advice to small business owners. www.score.org.

Small Business Development Centers. SBDC represents America's nationwide network of Small Business Development Centers. They attempt to help new entrepreneurs realize the dream of business ownership, as well as help existing businesses remain competitive. www.Americassbdc.org.

Young Entrepreneur Council. YEC is an organization for entrepreneurs ages 40 and under. It is an invite-only organization that assists with all aspects of business by offering a variety of products and services.
https://yec.co.

Micro Mentor. This is a service that allows entrepreneurs to get free advice from an expert in their free community of vendors. www.micromentor.org.

Women Venture. Women Venture provides women with the tools and resources to achieve economic success through small business ownership. www.womenventure.org.

The Kauffman Foundation. The Kauffman Foundation works to advance entrepreneurship education and training, to promote start-up friendly policies, and to understand what new firms need. www.kauffman.org.

U.S. Department of Veterans Affairs: The Veteran Entrepreneur Portal (VEP) is designed to make it easier for small businesses to access Federal services. VEP offers direct access to the resources necessary to guide every step of entrepreneurship. https://www.va.gov/osdbu/entrepreneur/.

National Association of Women Business Owners: NAWBO is an organization for women entrepreneurs that provides an outlet for women business owners to share their creativity, inspire, and support each other. www.nawbo.org.

Many people have paved the way and provided the blueprint for success. Most successful people are more than happy to share their knowledge and experiences with those who are eager to learn. Instead of reinventing the wheel, seek these individuals out. They may have priceless information that can help make your business a success.

7

SOCIAL MEDIA AND YOUR BUSINESS

With the click of a mouse, your website can be viewed by millions of people around the world. A savvy businessperson understands this and seeks new and creative ways to stand out in order to increase their website traffic and internet presence.

The internet is also a great way to make money every month just from people visiting your site. In this section, we'll discuss how the use of the internet can generate income, even if a person doesn't purchase your products.

Your Website: Worth its Weight in Gold

In 2015, the International Telecommunication Union estimated that approximately 3.2 billion people (or half the world's population) would be online by the end of the year. Getting some of this internet traffic should be your goal when you create a website. Here are the top tips for creating a website that will attract visitors:

Rich content. You must give people a reason to visit your site. That means having quality content that will keep them interested and wanting to stay after they find your page.

Create a blog. Write weekly posts about trends in your industry or something that can capture your reader's attention, wanting to come back for more.

Quality design. Your site must be pleasing to the eye. Loud colors or a hastily made site that looks unprofessional will turn viewers off and give them the impression that the business is unprofessional as well.

Make it interactive. Give your clients something to do by making it interactive. Include videos of you or your business for them to view. Offer a newsletter or email subscription to ensure you can keep in contact with them.

Easy to navigate. Add easy-to-use links on each page so viewers can navigate your site quickly and efficiently. The harder a site is to navigate, the quicker they will leave, never to return.

Mobile friendly. 60% of the world's population currently has a mobile phone, and it is estimated that 5 billion people will have mobile phones by 2019. It is important to have a website that is compatible with mobile devices (phones and tablets) so you can reach as many people as possible.

Fast load times. People are impatient, and if a page takes too long to load, they will quickly move on to another site. Consider these statistics:

- A one second delay in page load times yields 11% fewer page views.[5]

- Amazon.com reported increased revenue of 1% for every 100 milliseconds improvement to their site speed.[6]

- 40% of users will abandon a website if it takes more than three seconds to load.[6]

- 52% of online shoppers say fast page loads are important for their loyalty to a site.[6]

Having a website that is slow to load can cost you money. Here are ways to ensure faster load times on your website:

1. **Enable browser caching.** This allows a computer to store the elements of your page for future reference. This will allow for faster load times.

2. **Optimize images.** Larger images take longer to load, so consider using smaller images that viewers can click on to enlarge. JPEG images are quicker to load, while GIFs can take several seconds.

3. **Keep plugins on your site to a minimum.** Plugins are software add-ons that are installed onto programs to give them additional features. While plugins are popular, they can make your site run slow and can even cause crashes. Delete all unnecessary plugins and check for those that slow down your site.

4. **Reduce URL redirects.** Redirects occur when a person visits a web page and it changes to a different URL instead. These redirects create additional HTTP and increase load time. HTTP stands for Hypertext Transfer Protocol. This is the underlying protocol used by the World Wide Web. It defines how messages are formatted and transmitted,

and what actions Web servers and browsers should take in response to various commands. (We often see HTTP at the beginning of website addresses.)

One way to decrease the risk of redirects slowing your site is by using a HTTP redirect that sends mobile users directly to the mobile equivalent URL without any additional redirects.

By speeding up your site, you can attract more visitors to your site and provide a positive experience for your visitors.

The Importance of Search Engine Optimization (SEO)

Having a great website is important, but it's all for naught if people don't know it exists. Understanding what SEO is and how it works is essential to your success.

SEO is how your website is found via search engines like Bing, Yahoo and Google. When people search using keywords, the goal is to have your site among the top sites listed. This draws more attention to your site and hopefully means more business. Here are the top ways to increase your SEO optimization:

Use Keywords: People tend to search using phrases or keywords. By including certain phrases that pertain to your business throughout your site, you increase the probability of being seen by more visitors. The best keywords are based on the following guidelines:

- Avoid single word keywords because they are ineffective.

- Choose phrases that are pertinent to your business, but not too broad. For example, "computer repair" is broad, but "inexpensive laptop computer repair in Chicago" is more specific.

- Avoid terms that are too popular or common. The idea is to stand out from the crowd, not blend in with it.

Have a catchy page title. The title is the first thing customers notice when searching online. Using keywords in the title helps to improve the SEO as well. Please note: some search engines show 60 characters or less in their title tags, so make sure it's not too long.

Update content regularly. Sites with new and exciting content on a consistent basis rank higher on SEO than those with fewer updates. Look at it from the client's perspective: which site would you rather visit, the site with a new update this week, or the site that has been inactive for 2 months?

Focus on your URL. Search engines often gravitate toward short and catchy. Make sure the URL is relevant to the topic at hand.

Avoid using flash. Flash sites tend to rank lower in SEO because they may not be linked to an individual page.

The internet is used 24 hours a day, 7 days per week. Increase your SEO ranking and capture some of that web traffic. There are also ways to make money from the website traffic as well. We will discuss this in the next section.

Advertising Revenues: Monetizing Your Website

One of the goals of having a website is to generate business. This is a great way to expand your reach to people you may never meet. What if your website generates traffic but the people who visit don't purchase your goods and services? A great way to use this to your advantage is by monetizing your site.

When a site is monetized, a monthly income stream can be created from people simply visiting the site. This is accomplished by placing advertisements from various companies on your website. Here is a brief breakdown of the top ways to monetize your website:

Cost per click (CPC). These are ads placed on your site that pay-per-click. In other words, if a person clicks on the ad, you receive a commission even if they do not purchase anything. Google AdSense and media.net are two popular CPC options.

CPM Advertising Networks. These ads pay per 1,000 page views. Value Click Media and Tribal Fusion are popular CPM companies.

Affiliate Networks. These ads pay a percentage of the sale if someone purchases something via the link on your site. Amazon, eBay and iTunes all offer affiliate programs for interested websites.

Sell your products. Books, e-books, video training courses and exclusive membership sections are ways to make money on your site as well.

Sell ad space directly. Selling ad space to businesses in your area is another viable option.

Here are a few tips on monetizing your website.

Increase traffic. The key with monetizing your site is visitors. The more visitors a website has, the more revenue it can generate. Aim for a minimum of 500 visitors per day.

Ad placement. Place the ads in sections where

visitors will see them: near the top, on the side, in the middle of the page, and at the bottom

Choose ads that are similar to your site theme. For example, if you have a health and fitness website, a person may find your site after doing a search for health-related products, fitness classes or exercise tips. Books on healthy eating, vitamins, sports equipment, essential oils, water and other fitness themes are sensible options for ads. If a person found your site via a specific search, there is a great chance they will purchase a product on your site that matches their search criteria.

By taking advantage of every option available, you can increase your chances of success (and make a profit doing it).

8

THE ART OF PROFESSIONALISM

We have discussed many important tips for starting a successful business, but there are two rules that must never be broken:

1. Treat *all customers* with respect.
2. Remain professional at *all times.*

No matter how good a product is, if either of these rules are broken, your business is certain to fail. Let's go over each in detail:

1.   Treat all customers with respect.

One of the most important rules to remember is to never take your customers for granted. This is especially true for start-ups. When starting a business, a person will often solicit business in one or more of the following ways:

- Asking family and friends for support

- Advertise as a new business (grand opening)

- Support business themes (buy American, buy black, buy local, etc.)

While customers are initially happy to oblige and show their support, it is imperative not to rely on these types of "sympathy sales" to sustain your business. This is a great way to get people to check out your business for the first time, but there is no guarantee this will cause them to return.

We all had the unfortunate experience of being asked to support a business that was unprofessional and had poor products and/or service. While we did our civic duty, we never patronized them again. In some cases, the business owner thought their customers were obligated to spend money with them.

Do not have this mindset.

The average consumers are looking for value and quality. They are not obligated to patronize your establishment "just because." Instead of hoping they spend their hard-earned money based on sympathy sales, ensure they return because you have the best product available. Many relationships have been strained because business owners expected their family and friends to support them, but they chose not to.

Just because a person starts a business does not mean people should patronize it. Give them a reason to spend their money. Provide a service they feel they can't live without. No one owes you anything and if you want people to buy your product, make it the best product available. Period.

2.   Remain Professional at All Times

One of the fastest ways to lose customers is to be disrespectful and lack professionalism. Here are some of the most common traits of an unprofessional business:

Tardiness. Being consistently late for client meetings or appointments is a great way to lose business. No one likes to waste time. Tardiness will give the impression you do not take your work seriously. Make an effort to arrive 5-15 minutes early for appointments.

Unprofessional communication. If clients reach out to you, make an effort to respond quickly. The more time it takes to respond, the more time it gives your customer to spend their money elsewhere. Talking down to prospective clients is also unacceptable. Treat every customer as if they are your best customer. Common courtesy can lead to positive reviews on social media, which can generate more sales.

Lack of quality work. Take pride in your work. Make sure it is professional and completed correctly the first time.

Not being accountable. If the client is unhappy, don't make excuses. Make an effort to rectify the problem quickly and without delay. Arguing or disagreeing with a client will only hurt you in the long run. All it takes is one negative post on social media and the damage to your reputation is done.

Professional appearance. Unless a person is a mechanic, plumber, or another similar profession, a clean, professional appearance is a must. This also applies to the work environment. A sloppy appearance gives the impression that your business is not to be taken seriously. A potential customer can decide they will not work with you just on appearance alone. Without speaking a word, clients can be lost, and the confused entrepreneur will never know what happened.

Here are several ways to maintain a professional appearance:

- Keep your clothes and shoes in good condition.
- Avoid wearing wrinkled clothing.
- Have a fast website with no grammatical errors.
- Keep your work vehicles clean and running well at all times.

The smallest things can make a big difference in business. Do not give your customers a reason to dislike you before you say hello.

In the next chapter, we will discuss various aspects of cash flow and your business. The success of any business invariably comes down to how the money is managed.

9
NO DISCOUNTS: PERCEPTION IS EVERYTHING

For many new business owners, there is an intense desire to get as many clients or customers as they can. Many new business owners may be tempted to offer steep discounts or sales to generate business.

This is a big mistake.

There have been many studies conducted on the purchasing habits of consumers, and one trait has been constant across the board: the higher the price, the higher the quality and perceived value. On the flipside, as the price drops, so does the perceived value. This is especially important for business owners that provide a service.

Case I

U2 is arguably one of the most famous bands in the world, selling out arenas on every continent. However, one day in 2015, the group performed a few of their songs in a New York subway station while in disguise. What do you think happened?

They were ignored.

The band U2 was performing a FREE concert in a New York subway station, and they barely got a second glance as people walked by. It wasn't until they took off their disguises and revealed who they were that people took notice and pandemonium erupted.

Case II

In a classic study on painkillers, researchers offered test subjects two painkillers: one was selling at the full price of $2.50 per pill and the other was discounted to 10 cents each. Researchers applied electrical shocks to the wrists of study participants before and after they had taken the pain pills. Their findings:

- 85% of the patients who took the more expensive pill felt a reduction in pain from the shocks

- 61% of those who took the lower priced pill felt a reduction in pain

The test subjects did not know both pills were identical. They were actually given a placebo, NOT pain medication.

Case III

A study was conducted on energy drinks by Baba Shiv, Professor of Marketing at Stanford Business School. One group of study participants paid full price for energy drinks that claimed to make them feel more alert and energetic after consumption. Others were given the same energy drinks at a discounted price. Participants were then asked to solve a series of word puzzles.

The results were surprising: In all three studies, those who paid discounted prices solved fewer puzzles than those who paid full price, even though the drink was identical.

Other studies have been conducted on other products as well. For example, wine drinkers enjoyed wine that was considered vintage and more expensive. Perception is everything, and this is especially true when it comes to running a business.

Looking at U2 again, why would people pay hundreds of dollars to see them in a stadium that holds 60,000 people, but walk past them on a subway? It comes back to the perception of quality. When people think of subway performers, they may assume the talent is not as good, or if they were any good, they'd be onstage charging hundreds of dollars.

This is obviously untrue, but *perception* can have a greater influence on logic in many cases. By keeping your prices high, a person is more inclined to believe the product will outperform its lower priced counterparts, even if they are identical.

By discounting your listed price, consumers may subconsciously believe that your product is inferior and you do not believe in your own product. They could subconsciously lower their expectations on the effectiveness or quality of your service when the price is discounted. Countless studies have proven this to be the case.

In order to have satisfied customers, they must feel good about the decisions they make. These decisions aren't based on logic; they are based on emotion. Most purchases are made based on emotion, and it's important for business owners to understand this. Tapping into the emotional side of purchasing decisions is key.

There are several ways to make the consumer feel

good. Many of the principals previously outlined in this book can increase the perception of quality, but here are a few more:

1. **Create a good product.** This is key. As prices rise, so do expectations. Make sure your product is just as good (if not better) than the products currently on the market. It must be reliable, durable, and able to outperform the competition.

2. **Have great features.** What can the product do? Can it make a person feel good? Help them feel safer? How does it make them feel? Logically, we know a $20,000 car is probably safe and reliable, but how does a person feel when getting into that $20,000 car versus that fancy new car that cost $80,000? Do they feel the same?

3. **Physically appealing.** Mercedes and BMW are two of the most popular auto manufacturers in the world. One reason is because their vehicles simply look good. Packaging is very important when it comes to perception. If you take the time to make your product look good, the perception is that it must be good as well. Ask yourself: if you have two Christmas gifts in front of you, one is wrapped impeccably with expensive paper and a fancy

71

bow, while the other is wrapped with newspaper and electrical tape, which would you open first?

4. **Self-confidence.** If you KNOW you have a great product, you will act accordingly. On the other hand, a person who does not believe in their product (or themselves) will project those feelings onto their customers, and they will sense it from a mile away. If you don't believe in yourself or your product, why should anyone else?

5. **Responsiveness.** Respond quickly to customer concerns and be willing to answer all questions about your product, no matter how difficult. This increases the perception that you care about them and more importantly, you stand behind your product. If your customers can't reach you, they may start to think *"what are you hiding? Why are you avoiding me?"*

6. **Create an experience.** Make your customer feel good by working with you. Compare shopping experiences at high-end stores or restaurants to those at discount department stores or restaurants that serve value meals. The products might be similar, but the experiences and feelings consumers feel when

visiting these establishments are remarkably different.

By changing the perception of your business, you can demand a higher price for your services and people will pay accordingly.

10

LOGIC VS. EMOTION

Many business owners try to use logic when influencing consumers to buy their products, but studies indicate that emotion is the biggest factor. Many decisions are based on emotion, not logic. Logically, a modest home or nondescript sedan is all we need to survive, but emotionally, we want much more. We want the bells and whistles. We want to feel good about our purchase.

Logically, we know if we're in a bad relationship breaking up is the right thing to do, but emotionally, it can be extremely difficult to carry it through. These same thought processes occur when making purchases.

A smart business owner understands this and attempts to reach his customers via emotion, not logic.

There are several emotions that drive consumers to make purchasing decisions:

Regret. This consumer believes if they do not buy now, they may regret it later.

Pride. If they buy it now, they believe they will look smart and earn the respect and admiration of their peers.

Fear. If they don't make the decision now, it could hurt them in the long run.

Humanity. If they buy your product, they can help others.

Competition. If they don't buy now, their competitors/enemies will be one step ahead and win.

These emotions will not apply to every business of course, but some variations of these emotions may influence their buying decision. For example, competition probably won't prompt a person to get an oil leak repaired on their car, but fear or regret will. Humanity may not prompt a person to purchase this book, but trying to stay ahead of their competition might.

In addition to the above emotions, the following words in advertising and conversation can evoke emotional responses to help entice customers to buy your product:

- *There's more*
- *Worried*
- *Tough*
- *Hard*
- *Right now*
- *Maybe*
- *Better*
- *End*
- *Guarantee*
- *Results*
- *Proven*
- *Love*
- *Safe*
- *Safety*
- *You*

The shorter the words or phrases, the more emotion they can generate.

As you look at your business, ask yourself the following questions:

1. *What emotions do I want my customers to experience while working with me?*
2. *How do I want my customers to feel after doing business with me?*
3. *How long do I want them to feel this way after we have finished conducting business?*

The key is to know your customers and what will prompt them to make purchases. By increasing the perception of your products, you can be one step closer to making a sale and being a successful business owner.

In other words, you're not in the business to sell products; you're selling emotional connections. In the words of author Simon Sinek, *"People don't buy what you do, they buy why you do it."* With that said, don't make the mistake of sacrificing quality for the sake of emotions. If your product is subpar, those positive emotions can quickly turn into feelings of anger and resentment. If your product is outstanding AND you tap into their emotions, you increase your chances of having a successful business.

11

TAX WRITE-OFFS

Starting and operating a successful business takes a lot of time, effort, and most importantly, money. Most small business owners use their own money to get their business up and running. To help ease some of the pain, the IRS allows for certain items to be used as tax deductions for business expenses:

Home office. A portion of home personal expenses are deductible, provided the home is used regularly and exclusively as a place of business. Available deductions include direct costs such as painting or repairing a home office, and indirect costs, such as a percentage of rent or real estate taxes.

Car and truck expenses. The cost of operating your vehicle for business purposes can be deducted if records are acquired indicating it was used as such. Another option business owners have is to use the IRS standard of mileage, which was 57.5 cents per mile in 2015 instead of itemizing deductions.

Insurance. Malpractice coverage, business continuation insurance and the cost of your business owner's policy are fully deductible.

Supplies. Items that are used for your business are completely deductible.

Utilities. Electricity for your facility is fully deductible.

Meals and entertainment. These costs (such as a business lunch or dinner) are 50% deductible.

Taxes. State and local taxes charged for goods and services can be deducted. Licenses, regulatory fees, and taxes on real estate and personal property can be deducted as well.

Repairs. Repairs to business equipment are fully deductible.

Mortgage interest. Mortgage interest can be fully deducted for businesses that own realty.

Contract labor. Independent contractor usage is deductible, but additional paperwork may be needed to process when taxes are filed.

Advertising. Ordinary advertising costs are fully deductible.

Depreciation. The cost of buying property for your business is deductible. It also includes a deduction for equipment purchases up to $500,000.

Qualified Retirement Plans. Contributions to qualified retirement plans for self-employed individuals are personal deductions that are claimed on Form 1040. On the other hand, employee benefit programs such as contributions to employee qualified retirement plan accounts are deductible.

Travel expenses. If going out of town on business, lodging and transportation costs are fully deductible. This only applies to out of town travel. Local commuting costs are not deductible under travel expenses.

Mileage. This is a huge deduction, the key to the mileage deduction is you must keep track of your mileage records.

Legal fees. Legal and accounting fees are fully deductible.

These are the most common business deductions,

but there are more available for business owners. It's also important to note that unlike individuals who only file once a year, small business owners are responsible for making quarterly estimated tax payments each year.

Also, it is strongly advised to consult with a tax advisor to take full advantage of the tax laws available to you. Tax laws can change as well, so it's important to stay abreast of what is available to you. A great source of information is the IRS website www.IRS.gov.

12

SAVING FOR RETIREMENT

The goal of a business is to make money, but what should a person do with it once they have it? It is estimated that 70% of entrepreneurs aren't contributing to a retirement plan, and 28% aren't saving at all.[8] Having a nest egg and saving for retirement are two things we all should have. Entrepreneurs have several options when it comes to saving for their golden years, and here are the most popular savings options specifically for them.

Please note: the contribution rates may change. Please visit www.irs.gov for additional information.

1.   **Simplified Employee Pension (SEP).** A SEP IRA allows an individual to contribute as much as

25% of your net self-employment income, up to a maximum $49,000.

Pros: The account does not have to be funded until tax returns are filed.

Cons: If employees are hired, money put into the plan counts as an employer contribution. All "covered" workers who meet the following criteria must receive the same percentage contribution:

- Over the age of 21

- Employed by you for at least three of the last five years

- Expected to earn $550.00 in the current year

2.   **Solo 401 (k).** This retirement plan is popular among business owners and their spouses who can set aside large amounts of the earnings. Employees can save $16,500, and employers can save 25% of compensation, or $49,900, depending on their employee contribution.

Pros:

- Monies can be rolled in from a previous employer's 401(k) plan

- Can take out a loan against a solo 401 (k)

Cons:

- The employee contribution limit is maxed out at a combined $16,500/$22,000 employee contribution limit, regardless of how many jobs or 401(k) plans a person has.

3. **Simple IRA.** The Savings Incentive Match Plan for Employees is specifically designed for small businesses and self-employed individuals with fewer than 100 employees. The annual contributions are limited to $12,500, with catch-up contributions of $3,000 for those over the age of 50.

Pros:

- Easy to establish

Cons:

- Can't contribute if you already maxed out a 401(k) from your employer

- 25% penalty if making withdrawals within two years of inception.

Other plans:

Defined Benefit Plans. This is a pension plan which focuses on the payout at retirement, not the annual contributions. The business owner decides how much they want to be paid in retirement, and the minimum funding levels are then calculated. The maximum annual amount that can be received annually is $215,000.

Profit Sharing Plan. This plan simply lets you decide how much you want to contribute on an annual basis. The maximum amount is up to 25% of compensation (minus contributions for yourself) or $53,000.

Money Purchase Plan. This plan requires a fixed percentage of your income to be contributed annually, with a limit of 25% of compensation (not including contributions for yourself).

Here is a handy chart to compare the various plans side by side:

Plan FAQ	401(k)	Simple IRA	SEP IRA
Who Can Contribute	• Employee • Employer optional	• Employee • Employer	• Employer only; must make equal contributions for employees
Maximum Employee Contribution	$18,000 plus $6,000 catch-up if over 50 years old	$12,500 plus $3,000 catch-up if over the aged of 50	N/A
Early Withdrawal Penalty	• 10% early withdrawal penalty • penalty free loans	• 25% penalty for withdrawals within first 2 years of plan • 10% after 2 years	• 10% penalty for early withdrawal
Employer Contribution	• Up to 25% of earnings capped at $53,000k • Up to $58,000 if over the age of 50	• Must match 100% of first 3% of participating employee contributions or 2% of all eligible employee salaries	• Employer only contribution up to 25% of income or compensation with a $53,000 cap

These numbers are subject to change from the IRS at any time. A financial adviser or tax preparer should be consulted before choosing a retirement plan.

13

INVESTMENT OPTIONS

Once a small business owner decides which investment vehicle is right for their situation, they can then decide on how they want their monies to be invested inside the plan. Here are the most common investment options:

Mutual funds. Mutual funds are investment vehicles comprised of monies collected from a large group of investors. These monies are then invested into stocks, bonds, money markets, and other assets. There are many types of mutual funds:

1. **Money-market funds.** These funds are considered safe, but they cannot guarantee a

profit or loss. These funds invest in short-term, fixed income securities such as government bonds, treasury bills and certificates of deposit. They generally have a low rate of return.

3. **Fixed income funds.** Also, known as bond funds, these funds focus on investments that offer a fixed rate of return, hence the name "fixed." Government bonds and corporate bonds are the most common assets found in these funds. These funds seek investments that generate interest on a consistent basis. They are riskier than money-market funds, but not as risky as equity funds.

4. **Equity funds.** Equity funds invest primarily in stocks. These funds are the riskiest, but they also can generate the greatest reward. There are different classes of equity funds as well. Here are a few:

   • **Growth funds.** These funds focus on companies that are growing faster than average.

   • **Large cap funds.** These funds invest in larger, more established companies. Coca-Cola, Procter & Gamble, and Ford are examples of large cap investments.

- **Small cap funds.** Smaller companies with lower revenues but high growth prospects are chosen for these funds.

- **Specialty funds.** These funds focus exclusively on companies in the certain sector. Technology (tech) funds and pharmaceutical funds are examples of specialty funds.

- **Index Funds.** These funds track the performance of stock market indicators. The value of the fund will mimic the fluctuations of the actual index. Dow Funds and S&P 500 funds are examples of index funds.

5. **Specialty Funds.** These funds will focus on other investments, such as real estate, or commodities, such as gold, silver, or oil.

Think of your retirement plan as an umbrella, and how you invest your money as being under the umbrella. For example, if your retirement plan of choice is a 401(k), the mutual funds and stocks you purchase are under the umbrella, and inside your 401(k).

Many small business owners opt to use a financial advisor to manage their investments, but it's important to have a basic understanding of how investing works and how your money is invested.

14
CLOSING REMARKS

Many people want to start their own business, but they are afraid. They are afraid of the unknown. They are afraid of failure. They are afraid of stepping out of their comfort zone. Make no mistake, running your own business is A LOT of work. There will be long days and sleepless nights. There will be days you wonder why you're doing this, and if things will ever get better.

There are few guarantees in life, and no one can promise that your business will be successful. There's a chance it will fail, but what if it doesn't? What if you beat the odds and become successful beyond your wildest dreams?

Regret is one of the worst feelings in the world. Few things are worse than looking back on your life and wondering "what if." Personally, I would rather try than not try at all. At least then I know. I can rest easy knowing I at least tried and gave it my best shot.

Starting a business is similar to having kids: few of us are ever ready, and none of us know what will happen. We learn as we go, but most parents would say they are happy with their decision to have kids and have no regrets. It's the same with your business.

Your business is your baby. It's your job to nurture it and help it grow. Like kids, business can be very unpredictable, but that's what makes life worth living.

Too many of us have jobs we don't enjoy and we're just go through the motions, waiting for the weekend. Our livelihoods are in someone else's hands, and we are scared to death of getting laid off. We search the job ads, hoping to find a job we like that pays well and is close to home. Sometimes, we will relocate just for that job.

Some of us don't have a formal education and feel this is preventing us from getting a job or doing what we want to do. While a formal education or degree is needed for some professions like a doctor or dentist, it's not needed for all professions.

The following successful business owners didn't complete a formal education:

Steve Jobs. Steve Jobs dropped out of Reed College, yet he was the co-founder of Apple with Steve Wozniak, also a college dropout. At the time of his death, Mr. Jobs was worth $11 billion.

Richard Branson. Richard Branson dropped out of high school at 16 but went on to create Virgin Airways, Virgin Records, and Virgin Mobile. He is now worth $4.9 billion.

Dave Thomas. Dave Thomas is the founder of Wendy's. He dropped out of high school to work at the Hobby House restaurant. At the time of his death, his net worth was $99 million.

Larry Ellison. Larry Ellison is the founder of Oracle. He dropped out of not one, but two colleges. Currently, he is currently worth $48.3 billion.

Rachael Ray. Rachel Ray never attended college, but that did not stop her from becoming an author and TV star. She is reportedly worth $66 million.

We are *not* saying or suggesting for you to quit college or that college is a waste of time. We are simply saying that no matter who you are or what your educational level is, you CAN become a successful business owner. The key is to learn everything you can about your profession and work harder and smarter. By using the principals in this book, you can be well on your way to making your dreams come true.

In 2015, employers announced close to 500,000 job layoffs, a 36% jump over 2015 and a 2% increase over 2014.[9] It's time to make a stand. It's time to take control of your life and your destiny. It's time to do something YOU like. It's time to be an inspiration to others and create something that can be passed down to the next generation.

Don't wait for someone to help you or give you their blessing. What if that help never comes? Don't be afraid to take a leap of faith due to fear.

Not everyone is meant to be an entrepreneur, and that's ok. But if you're reading this that means you are either running your own business now or seriously contemplating it. This book simply gives tips on getting started and is intended to give you the best chance to succeed. Nothing is guaranteed, but we must try. Don't wait for someone to give you a job. Discover how to establish your own job and create a legacy by applying these principals.

Need help? I am determined to help you succeed! I am available for a free 30 minute consultation. Let's talk and see how we can make your business become a success! Are you *Readi? Time to get Set. Ok, Let's Go!*

We wish you the very best on your small-business endeavors!

ABOUT THE AUTHORS

Stephanie A. Wynn is a seasoned entrepreneur who possesses 20 years of Financial Services experience. She is the founder of Wynn & Wynn Business Solutions, LLC, a business consulting firm located in St. Petersburg, Florida. Stephanie is passionate about assisting entrepreneurs with establishing and re-branding their small businesses. She is committed to giving back to the less fortunate and making a difference in the lives of others. Contact Stephanie for a free 30 minute consultation today. She can be reached via her website www.stephanieawynn.com.

Jeffrey White is a former financial advisor turned wellness coach, personal trainer, and motivational speaker. He is the owner of Jeff White Fitness Solutions LLC. and graduated from Illinois State University with a degree in Business Administration. He is the author of *Success Principles 101: A Step By Step Guide on Setting and Achieving Your Goals* and the Amazon Best Seller and award-winning book, *The 3 Pillars of Strength: Increasing Your Physical, Mental, and Spiritual Fitness*. Jeffrey lives in Tampa, Florida with his wife Monica and son Little Jeffrey. Jeffrey can be reached for consultations via his website:

www.JeffWhiteFitnessSolutions.com.

INDEX

[1]A Business Plan Doubles Your Chances for Success.
https://smallbiztrends.com/2010/06/business-plan-success-twice-as-likely.html

[2]Radware Report Reveals Slow Websites Will Cost Retailers Big Bucks this Holiday Season
https://www.radware.com/newsevents/pressreleases/summer-sotu2015/

[3]Global Internet Usage.
https://en.m.wikipedia.org/wiki/Global_Internet_usage

[4]Number of mobile phone users worldwide 2013-2019 Statista
https://www.statista.com/statistics/274774/forecast-of-mobile-phone-users-worldwide/

[5]Aberdeen Group.
http://www.aberdeen.com/Aberdeen-Library/5136/RA-performance-web-application.aspx

[6]Akami.com press release.
http://www.akamai.com/html/about/press/releases/2009/press_091409.html

[7]The Behavioral Impact of a Higher Price | Stanford Graduate School of Business.
https://www.gsb.stanford.edu/insights/behavioral-

impact-higher-price

[8]Retirement Savings Plans for Entrepreneurs.
http://www.money-guy.com/2015/03/retirement-plans-entrepreneurs/

[9]Here's How Many Jobs U.S. Companies Cut in September.
http://fortune.com/2015/10/01/layoffs-jobs-september/

Readi- Set Go!

101

Made in the USA
Lexington, KY
01 April 2017